kachina

Our lives look out
from a green tangle
of vines,
a cave reached by rope
ladders. We see
the nightly
beacons
spinning moon chips
thru a waterfall.
We are drawn,
for our fires are never
warm enough, our sons
die with one night's
fever, the forest feeds
with many teeth
on our firm bodies.
We are drawn by distant
sounds of laughter
like glass breaking
and we hear
a music whose notes die
on our air.

All this they mark,
but they do not go forth
for their gods are strong
who come like new wives
to their beds in the dark.

kachina

By John Perlman

OHIO STATE UNIVERSITY PRESS

811.54
P42K
80952
nov. 1972

To Wanda Ingmier,
To John Hott,
To My Wife, Jan and
daughter, Nicole —

love.

CONTENTS

LE DOUANIER

RACIAL MEMORY

THE NATURE OF THE PLACE

ACKNOWLEDGMENTS

Some of the poems have appeared in *Haiku Highlights, Escutcheon,* and *First Issue #4.*

le douanier

**Le Douanier
Answers
His
Critics**

Often, my poor wife's praise guides my hand.
With our small pension, we are quite content.
Even Apollinaire, when I measured
The precise distances of his face,
Thought such a simple life
A fitting justification for my art,
Though he believed my eye trained
In the Mexican jungle, the thin air
Brushing light on the undersides of shadows,
Foliating my dreams. For that
I had no answer. Painting, with more rules
Than government service,
Reveres the balances of nature.
While I paint a soil beyond my studio,
I trace only the possible.

"The
Repast
of
the
Lion"

No, the sun neither rises
Nor sets at the mountainside;
Flowers, too blue, too pink,
Will not wither into seed;
No apes to peel
Bananas of the goldest gold;
The jungle is not ageless,
Unending, not the tangled
Spirit, realm of the giant fern;
No snakes lurk in unseen bogs;
No spiders with ready webs;
No drums reveal a savage doom.
Yet the lion must have meat
And will find it where he can.

"Storm
in
the
Jungle"

Though the stiff grass snaps your legs
As you pass, and the rain pecks
Like gnats at your back, the trees
Bow in the wind before you.

No power swivels in his throne
Condemning your smug regency,
Or mimics your terror to his court.
Your tired wish to flee the forest

Drives you out. The thunder
Shivers in your fur. Wet leaves
Tumble past the soft, swift
Padding of escape. Never believe

Brilliant, dark men at the edge of the red
Desert, enthralled at your coming,
Will honor your image, bringing
Sacred flesh, fire, or gold.

"The
Sleeping
Gypsy"

Too many nights a full belly
Numbing your dreams, the jungle
Withered as you slept. Your proud
Roar, like a dust-devil, rattled
The crisp leaves at your feet.
Grass puffed silence
In your ears. Vultures
Circled and were gone.

In your soft breath the gypsy dreams.
The mandolin awaits an aged hymn
Of passing hunger.

At the edge of the shallow lake
A yellow desert moon
Pauses full against the dawn.

"The
Snake
Charmer"

Pausing full against the dawn,
The silver jungle moon
Sleeps softly in the turning sky,
The deep lake drinks the rippling waves
Of sky waking into light.
To the passing of fear, the forest
Dances forth from shadow.
The lady has gone out from hiding
Her morning song,
Banished at the lion's roar,
Returns from memory. The dark snakes
Pay meek homage to her freedom. Flowers
Leap into bloom, they praise the sun in her eyes.

To
Sidney
Kaplan
1913–1967

(1)

On warm evenings, the peacocks
Preening, the flute often rustled
The hanging orchids. Shyly, the Gopis,
The magnet of Kama like the hot night wind,
Entered the forest, encircling
Their dark-eyed love.

(II)

The knife was cold to his hand,
But the flush of blood at his neck
Spun golden fire,
Round dark, green eyes,
Consuming forever pravasa.

To
My
Grandfather
Died
Jan. 13, 1969

The last few winters,
his circulation grew so weak
his hands froze in their gloves.
Cold-blooded feet
stubbing the sidewalk ice,
he often fell, once with his wife
into an empty shopping center fountain.

Once he sold a car
to Al Capone,
who paid in cash and shared
pictures of his family.
In 1929
he lost a fortune
in bank stock;
but met Roosevelt in the 30s
and caught a record muskie in Wisconsin.

Before he died, a great-granddaughter
was born. Every day
he slept later into the morning,
had soup for lunch
complaining the teeth hurt his gums.
Late in December
a vein broke through
the thin skin at his temple.
The neighborhood, used to seeing
an ambulance hurry
him away, nodded relief
at the slow turn it made
onto the highway, his wife
riding alone in the back.

At the funeral home,
I waited outside the chapel.
A great-aunt
complimented the way
his head was turned.
A young rabbi
said he must surely
have been well-loved.

Under an olive canopy,
standing on the packed cemetery snow,
I held my grandmother
in my arms, afraid
to look at my father,
and wept
for my wife and daughter,
300 miles away at home.

Aubade

It is bitter outside,
cars stall, toes like glass
ache dully, a bus idles
at a frozen corner.

Our attic room is small:
an afterthought window
sifts the early morning,
stopping a fitful wind,
passing light
focused by an iced sun
passing darts of cold
which shiver round the edges of our bed.

We lie facing,
sharing breath,
warm
like hands tightly held.

We are alone,
and your smile
wakes in my eyes.

Love
as
Artifact

It is such delicate craft,
Carving our love's twinning:
The wood hardens in the heat,
And the knife is chipped and dulled.
Still, it peeps awkwardly from the block,
Whirls its eyes in glee, flips
Its promised tail, flaps a wing.
Just a nip here, another slice,
A quick cut at the base. . . .
Suddenly the beak spurts flame
And we scurry with stone hatchets
Past the clearing to quarry another log.

Fear

Your hand trembled, holding
the gift. How

you studied the wrapping,
such soft care

in your thin fingers,
folding it, dry

in the flat dark
like the leaf we pressed

when no tree
grew for miles.

You can never, now,
open its lid.

As it waits on your dresser,
it sits here, on my desk.

We have traded
regret. I

think of you,
unfolding

this costly paper.

Less real
than a half-sleep,

an inconvenience
in my

bed, laughed at
by ceremonial

children, I
can't forget.

The graves
of my grand-

father, my
uncle, the

unpicked graves
of all

I love,
point east

to this house,
this bed.

I reach thru
the distant

flesh of my
wife, my

daughter. The
sun reddens,

grows, freezes
into space.

My hands curl
back

into their sleeves.

Advice   Do not hide your heart in a shell
              Where the sea is a rumor.

The
Victor

My own
sick sorrow:
what can
love
add?

The pure desire:
to give
the unique
gift.

Accommodation:
there are lesser
gifts
of some
value.

It is the second
lover

turns you,
spots the bedsheet,

laughs,
turns his back,

rests,
turns back

ready again.
Crazy

with desire
turn back

your eyes,
dig your nails

into his back.
Hard at work

taking his turn,
he won't hear

the door,
open and close,

open and close.

We loved carelessly,
As a boy who builds
A castle by the sea, then
Abdicates for dinner,
Returning to find his kingdom sacked
By a random wave.

Prayer
for
God's
Mercy
— to
Steve
Conklin

For the choking doubt
I offer death, I open
My hoarse chest,
Begging the old god
To splice my rib
Into her dull body.
Let each nerve transform
The love limping from my brain
To pulse in her hand
Fallen to the buzzing earth.
Dearest God, I have devoured
The snake and learned loss,
The apple shrivels in
Your dry sand,
The soft brook sizzles
In the hollows of these hot rocks.
Beyond brash clear sight, my eyes
Are forever blurred to her face.
On this final day of rest,
Rouse to these burning hills
The cool, wise heart
Whose love could never seek
To rival yours.

Georgen
(Gert)
Jessen
1919–1969

My uncle woke up
dead yesterday.
You can imagine the scene:
his wife, frantic,
holding him by the shoulders,
shaking him
until her fingers cramped.
Then, angry, confused,
a final slap. Think!
A phone call, something
to start him up again.
God, the kids,
this is no way, no way
to grow up. My uncle
lying there,
the covers tucked under his chin.
One can imagine the scene.

12/2/69

My
Swedish
Grandmother

She is old, older
than she wanted for
years. Runaway at

Fifteen, trained as a
cook, she married a
tailor, steel plate in

His knee, immigrant
to Ohio, struck
dead at fifty. Stays

In her daughter's home,
in her own room, pays
rent, babysits a

Great-granddaughter. No
one there to taste the
work, never cooks. Com-

Plains constantly, no-
where close to dying.

Dead
Letter
Office:
The
Sixties

It is now
ten years—

beside me
on this plane, two

businessmen expand
their Taiwan market—

the first ten
years I have had

to count.
I have become

human, my grandfather
my uncle

dead the same
year.

                I

pull back
my head, blowing

out my cheeks,
gaining

seconds. I never
conceived

the humanity
of ten years passing,

proving
time.

When the plane lands
my wife

will drive
home

through
a freezing rain.

The Taiwan market
could be worth

millions.

12/7/69

Matriarch   We saw her
             once.
             Her car stopped
             importantly
             in the driveway.
             Helped from the seat,
             she walked on air
             into the house, held
             up under both arms,
             sat in the heavy
             livingroom chair,
             and laughed
             royally
             at all of us.
             After dinner
             she left,
             retracing her steps.
             I guess
             she approved.

Evening   He walked up the hill,
along a driveway
covered with bright leaves
from a day-long wind.
He could see deeper
into the trees
than ever before,
but saw nothing moving.
In each step he thought,
"Tonight you will gain
neither lover nor friend
to be led, content
with expectation, along
this hillside, nothing
to break such solitude."
At the hilltop
a deer startled him.
At a safe distance,
they both stared.
When the deer turned,
he went inside the house.
He removed his coat
and built a fire
to burn until morning.

Marriage
Blues

The rent
three months overdue,
the landlord's wife
grows insistent.
This room is too small
to keep up, dishes
stop the sink, the floor
unswept, dusty.
I write little,
unopened bills
claim the desk-top.
My shelves are filled
with unread books.
In the evening, after work,
we have no time
to spend together.

Ode to My
Daughter
on the
Death of
Woodie
Guthrie

(I)

In the New York night,
Stung by brackish sleet,
He smiled—
Tonight he would write the sun into the sky.

(II)

Behind me on the floor my wife sleeps.
I fluffed a pillow for her head,
Brought a blanket
To tuck around her legs.
I rested my hand
On her round stomach.
She will pass this night,
Wake smiling and full, closer
To a fall which brings our child.

(III)

If hearing my song
On a bitter, empty night,
Will you think or know of a night
Your mother lay warm, asleep on the floor,
And your father,
Sad at Guthrie's death,
Wrote the sun into the sky
And his daughter into life?

3 A.M., awake
beyond sleep.

My daughter
coughs uneasily,

whining in her sleep.
My wife dreams

a private warmth.
And only

my burning eyes
have drifted off

to witness
the slight dawn

pulled into view.

Shaking
the
Butterfly
Mobile

Shaking the butterfly mobile
Which spots the fog above
Apprentice eyes,
My daughter smiles in privacy.

Here is no insect threat,
Hovering green, yellow, black bellies,
Tube-mouths like straws,
Prism-visioned hunger.

To dance, to color,
She has opened her eyes
To light. The first fumbling
Rift, a cocoon raveling

with private surprise.

The baby cries all day
In the heat of her first summer.
Through all her complaint
Relief is uncertain;
She will soon learn of another heat
That even her father
Cannot soothe.
What stranger comes then
To warm my house?

Pictures
of the
World
As She
Sees It

Nicole learns to end
her sentences with words,
gestures to match
a thousand tongues.
She matches all
the family parts,
though she smokes my pipe
like a bottle.
She even joins in the laughter.

Formal afternoons
soon after frost,
single trees
yellow on the hillside.
A squirrel
in the yard
turns its head.
Nicole on the swings
tumbles to the grass.
Scolding, Jan waves
sweaters from the door.
My pipe burns out
and warms a pocket
in my pants.
Dinner is ready.
Tonight, extra blankets
on the bed, an
untroubled
sleep.

(I)

A memory of poetry
bored

as an old Indian,
barely scrutable

to the thirsty tourists
in convertibles.

Crazy Horse, they say,
was blond.

(II)

A cop hit squarely
in the eye

picks up a plastic
bag of turds,

(in the papers, feces),
marked dietetic.

(III)

At eighteen, she has
already lost count.

Though some, usually married,
are better and last longer,

she worships the first.
They still get stoned together.

(IV)

Backs to the dust,
our mythic future

returns, covers
the stubble,

the politics
of the secular.

ὁ ἄγγελλος
— to
Frank
Samperi

(1)

The first bright Sunday,
we walked thru Charles St.
toward the river.
For weeks high clouds
had cooled the air
and closed windows.
Now even our coats
were heavy in the light wind.

Gulls grazed the swells.
Below the sun-glaze
we looked
into the empty water.

(2)

A black dog, nose
at a fan in the cotton grass.
Stiff, grave ladies with flowers,
with parasols. The sun out
over the river. Dark green
in the tree shadows.
In an orange dress, a girl
poised on one foot.
The island still.

(3)

Beautiful day, Mama, he said
to an old woman, leaning
from her window on a red pillow.
She smiled
but said nothing.

Presuppose   Though I endure
                  patience,
                  this must come
                  in my way
                  or not at all,
                  and if not at all . . .
                  the sunset fades
                  through
                  a slate sky—
                  slowly my eyes
                  smile out
                  at the visible dark.

racial memory

A
Dream
of
Indians

On all sides, scrub
oak on the valley floor, iron-
wood, wild grape, trunks
of thunder oak, gray beech.
Drifting off a rock face,
a waterfall. Dark
in the overhang, a fire
scaling the cliff. They sit
asleep on a circle of logs,
coming to their feet
slow as melting ice.
On a high ledge, a white
eagle spreads its wings
like a half moon.
They begin to turn,
circling the fire, inching forth.
At the light's edge, a wolf
sniffs the path. They face
the fire, bowing their heads,
joining arms, closing
their eyes. Above
the red coals, black
bears take the trees,
eagles perch on the air
like flames.

Racial
Memory

The Age of Reptiles
    Toward the end,
    Small mammals, cowering
    Under thick, extinct grasses
    Were hardly aware of
    Warmth in the blood; but,
    Finding an abundance of abandoned eggs,
    They persisted.

The Age of Man
    The swift, stabbing tongue
    Of a snake, a lizard's
    Hiss, call crashing thru the night,
    The promised thunder
    To splinter our huddled houses.

The
Growth
of
Myth

(I)

Poetry before all other arts
Objectifies the ineffable
Charting the swerving silhouettes
Of the sub-verbal.

(II)

As a hard freeze
Wedges onto the land,
A bent lady surveys the frightened village,
Her iced breath enshrouding the ground
Like phosphored snow.
The feast must be worthy,
She must acknowledge our prayers.

(III)

At the still mouth,
She warms the endless
Chill thinning her blood.
Her aged beak pecks
Calmly, her belly swelling
As at birth.

(IV)

Fateful Mother,
What was flesh is stone,
What was stone is water,
What was water is milk,
From your warm breast what is milk
Is flesh.
Take, Mother, this stone.
Let your hunger be ended,
So you may again suckle your children.

Failure

Offering boar's blood at the household altars
To gull the wary necromancers, we
Suckled their abandoned son,
Warning the servant at cost of his life
Would he tell of our pity.

Our scraping hills taught no subtlety
For fixing on the nearly good,
Or patience to await renegades
To people his mysterious temple;
They spoke only the ancient tale
Of his rightful throne
Just beyond the underbrush.

In the weakness of his youth, he saw huntsmen
Snapping cowls on his falcons
Who mauled velvet robes limping on croziers,
Dropping nets from ambush on his pumas
Who drew the hungry young behind a thicket;
Smiling, he sent the wild
To beat wide-eyed at their bedroom windows.

Know that though he now must speak
In an alien tongue,
His swelling strength is praise for those
Whom the animated wilderness now
Terrifies and must somehow seem
The vicious echoes
Of their careless failure.

To
John
Hott
in
Africa

Speak your discoveries
of a flesh taste to the
earth   and the damp
that leaves   no ruins
longer than a man's space.
For would you lay a man
and his city down together,
and the hyena   bare
his teeth above?
                    Shall the forest
rise to speak, when man
has fled the spot?
But the pace, the thump of
fear, padding the grass,
preys on the nomad.

Found there a home,
ancient and lush, in your keeping,
as the earth keeps you,
as you hear its pulse,
that your sons might be safe
at the foot of your bed,
your wife beside you.

Racial
Memory
II

Extinct Neanderthal,
In triumph,
Slit each wet bone
To lick at the marrow.
He buried food with his dead
And may have known faith.

If he had speech,
It is lost.
Thin as eggs,
The skulls collapsed.
Rock relieved
The scattered bone.

At the weak pulse
Of the vein,
We draw near
In antique thirst
A sacred word
To make death human,
The earth stir
At the sound.

As we sat
Beneath the shedding poplar,
Two seasons—Spring snow.

Leaf
Painting

A molten dune, sketched
Tentatively, stroke by stroke:
Fading pot of gold.

10/4/65

Aubade II   (I)

The dew chilled our bare feet
As Lady walked on waves of lawn,
Past my naïve paddling . . .

(II)

Night snow skids on a brittle floor,
Behind my puffing tongue
The runners of my sled scratch mockingly.

Drought —
for Bob W.

(I)

The scattered boulders, cracked
From the bank, balance uneasily;
A snake hosts flies in the sucking sun;
Slow fish huddle on the surface
Of a severed pond, waiting.

Curling through clogs of moss, a lure
Rests against the river,
Trailing a strip of split line,
Caught on a rock and nothing more;
A trout stares eyeless at the sky.

(II)

Seeing him for the last time,
The skin on his face was yellowed and dry;
His laughter treble like sobs;
His eyes narrowed, but deep and vacant.

He had mated a love
Who lay bored and impatient,
Swatting the flies that droned around her,
Draining his strength with indifference,
Leading him slyly in jest
Till he struck at the love and it snapped.

(III)

Slowly, we drink our beers
And wait, uneasily,
For something to happen.

Drought —
for Al W.

(I)

Like a sponge drying, the half-blown peach
Shrinks, as if, in desperation, the girdled tree
Must feed upon itself.

                   He cracked the attic window
With a chair, glass snapping like a whip,
And sledding down the roof, and slicing air.

(II)

Sliding through the trembling glass, blacking out the sun,
A lady in a velvet gown will seal what you've undone:
She'll ask you if your love was true,
While toying with your hair;
She'll slip beneath the sheets with you
And freeze you with a stare.
You must obey the words she speaks so softly as you sleep,
"Your love is as the swollen peach, and only yours to keep.
Go with clippers, swiftly go, snip it from the tree;
Hold it in your loving hand, bear it to the sea;
Let the sea flush round your feet,
Let your hair be wet;
Lift it to your lips and eat,
Promise to forget."

Chorus   Spitting phthisic phlegm
           In an aging, echoing house,
           Sounds quicken
           Like a child's ball bouncing,
           Swifter and ever softer until,
           As a barren conch to the ear,
           The static whispers of vague voices
           Chorus the rasp of silence.

City, #1   (I)

The lake in silent waves slides ashore
Upon a Sunday morning stilled in sleep,
Lapping below brown-stucco store fronts;
A dog, its hind leg hiked at a fire-hydrant;
And a ball game in an alley
Tearing past tufts of scrub grass,
Past the blast of a fan sucking from a grill
The warm scent of breakfast grease.

(II)

Our lungs inhale the shape of love:
Love like a vulture, awaiting his turn
In the pecking order, scanning the veldt
For carrion, or the trail of a lion;—
Like steam shooting from a sewer drain,
Melting an arc of snow, while a dog yellows
The white base of a hydrant and a drowsy
Child has fogged window above the alley.

(III)

The winter wind scratches its nails
At the panes of the city,
An old man,
His hand held forth
In supplication to museum gods.

On a
Geology
Field Trip—
Stop
One

The shale of this district
Is what? asks the gray professor,
Not expecting an answer
From the mixed, straining-serious
Group of undergraduates.

In a ravine of Big Run Creek
We struggle to picture that
Particular page
Of the supplementary textbook
Which plainly states, "Ohio Shale."

Yet, I'm distracted
By this well-known valley.
The shale resting by the point bar,
The four stepping stones of
Metamorphic gneiss,
And the sloping cliff of fallen talus,
Were skippers, a rock bridge
And an old Indian cliff—
When a few years ago,
We called this ravine The Ravine
And waged our endless wars
Of colonization and when
The only good Indian was a dead one
And . . .
   Page 101, showing the various types
Of area rocks
Including Ohio Shale . . .

Interrupts the sullen professor
In a programmed, dissecting voice,
While the purpose of learning
Settles like ether
On the unconvinced
Mixed group of undergraduates.

Uninvited, an heretical rock
Plops onto the regolith
By the teacher's muddy boots.
Looking up
With stern eyes
He beholds the enemy,
A tribe of boys
Who have suddenly
Sprung from behind ancient trees

At the top of the cliff,
Bombing the circle of students
With rocks of Devonian granite,
War-whooping, smiling,
Impregnable Head Indian Chiefs
At battle of Big Run Creek.

Muttering, the professor turns
To the snickering,
Part-time students,
Can anyone tell me . . .

Tribute to
Kenneth
Rexroth
and
Eli
Jacobson

With the lust of battle
The unwon war has passed.
Did you believe that as you fell
Joyfully we would take your place
On the cable, to taste the same
Sweat, slide the same block
Onto the summit of the same temple,
To the coming age?
Did you hate the faces
That mocked as you pulled,
The girls making love
Near the lines of march?
Could you feel other pain
As the dead blisters split?
As you fell, Jerusalem,
Like a floating island,
Cast off into space,
Toward planets hoarding living carbons
Wasted in the burning of your flesh.
The trailing light shimmers
With old age.

We are not blind
To what you have done.
At night, resting, eating,
We saw your smiles. The bread
You shared was a good taste
In our mouths. We swilled
The hidden flask, rushed
From hand to hand.

In the evening,
Sometimes bored,
We recall the faith of your age
And lights shine past the open
Doorways of our homes,
Friends drop in without knocking.

A Museum
Director
Soothes His
Actress-Wife
While Viewing
a Poorly
Preserved
Middle
Kingdom
Chieftan

This mummy's tight lips trace a laugh
furious at being suddenly frozen
in glee to await his souls.
Clutching the spear in your side and
screeching with balcony laughter
while your pants are soaked—
there is a better way to play death.

The fresh face of death should
pout like a fickle girl,
lips puffed forth in plastic despair,
subdued by silence.
Then perhaps your soul would know
who to look for.

Survived by
Parents
and
Wife —
To
Spike
Bonnell

An empty twitch in a soaked cot, he dies;
A scream clamped in his calmed lips,
His tongue sunken, sealing the throat like a vault,
Eyes spun by lids
Slammed like the gate at Hamlin's Hill.

Strung across a slipping fault,
They spring at tremors, a
Raw rattle of laughter
Testing the caulk;
At night the ceiling creaks
As silence waltzes on the roof.

She holds the deeper pain: mimic hands
That rudely grab her thighs,
Fear that pumps her breath;
Dangling above on strings,
The frantic surge of his finish
Quakes like a moth about the room.

At a rear door, sealing the dense mountain,
With a quiet smile the piper leaves,
Squashing an occasional
Pious mouse.

The
Diggings
at
Pompeii

In a narrow street
Near the palaestra,
By the marbled walls of a house
Buried in pumice,
The slack bones
Of a soldier
Spill a cup of wine.

Certainly the sickly gods
Had heard. A scholar,
Hard at work,
Restoring a frieze,
Finds, scribbled in bad latin,
The words:
To hell with empire.

Cavafy asleep, a young
Alexandrian curled against him,
Dreams in high Greek
Of low love.

In their warm fatigue,
He had kissed the ear
Of the strange, quiet boy, saying:
And he fell thunderously,
As a dark mist clouded
His eyes.

The Arab boy sleeps soundly,
And knows no Greek.

Pasiphae

By morning,
the gray run-off
through the gutter
has dwindled,
pooled with smoke
about the drain;

Curling blood
has corked
the trench
scooped
in Theseus' chest;

The sewer
carried
away
the thin ball
of twine;

Thoughtful Daedalus
has fled,
taking his son,
as the red
sunrise
brightens his handiwork.

In the cold
depth
of the grinding
black sea
cold fish
sleep
with wide-eyed
patience.

(1)

Will you have a simple
human truth?
The dead are also
made less each day.
For this, the priest
flutters his tongue
like a hawk in the wind
of his own
directed fear.
The long nails
embedded
in the cramped
small of your back
belong to no man's hand.

Now you, a familiar
with death's disembodied
service,
would shed the body
like an uncompromising skin.
Your taut grief alone
keeps you.
The shapes fear
decks a death out in—
a sightless hooded
owl, brown bats
creeping deaf thru the grass—
are innocent as you.
No man can
call them up,
they are
diffuse as breath
at the back of your neck.

(II)

In the fifteenth century
a well-preserved
aristocratic Roman girl
was unearthed near the Via Appia.
The countryside
was astonished. A rumor
that an oil lamp
miraculously still alight
had been found beside the body
drew the curious
from throughout the peninsula.
Except for a single breast,
her stomach and loins,
which had partially decayed,
she was perfect.

Pope Innocent, in fear
of wonder,
ordered the body taken
in the dead of night
and re-buried in secrecy
outside the Porta Pinciana.
Thus was lost "a sublimely
beautiful girl of noble family
from the days when Rome
stood at the pinnacle
of her glory."

(III)

Le Pere, the architect,
on first opening
the pyramid of Cheops:
A musty atmosphere
greeted us and we
became full of this
same unhealthy air. The
following night we fell
into such weariness and weakness
that within two days we
could stir
neither arm nor leg.

The
Rites
of
Mithra:
The
New
Year

"The Virgin has brought forth.
The light is waxing."
It is the still season
when old men die
softly in the early night
and grief settles on the household,
a three day snowfall.

Competing on the hilltops,
the fires are lit,
and children up late
this single night, break
low branches from
brittle trees. The fires
burn brighter
than the forest,
singe their laughter,
common as tinder.
Each stone is marked
and tossed, cold and careful,
into the fires of promise.

The light is waxing,
the sun has blazed
beyond the night.
In day's ashes
all stones are found,
all names revived.
Secure as dawn,
the Virgin has brought forth.
The old men smile into sleep,
passing over into dreams.

For Frank, Dolores, Claudia, and David

Here

If you look here for it,
it will not be here.
He smirks in the corner
of your eye. Frantic
turning starts him,
still at the corner.
There he brews his magic.
Even memory impinges
less obliquely.
Remember it. Here? It was not.

When you sleep
he wakes the lids
like an infant
tapping its fingers.
He is a free-fall
circling, wary
of light, focal and deadly.

He has hidden in
your closed hand,
sails at the thought,
tense below the palm.
Twist the fist open.
He drowses at the fringe
of your eye. If you
look here for it,
it will not be here.

The cars sink in the yard,
mud lipping each wheel.
Shadows scale the tops
of the grass blades, hover
to the cupped palms of the branches,
humming like crickets.
They are sweeping through each other
like bats, their wings catching at the finger-tips.
They have grown huge and tropical,
prey on all they fail to see.
Like mushrooms, the cars light the grass.
Shadows beat on the cracks in the windshields,
They ooze thru, the cars are racing.
Hurled together, throttled, they climb the night
like geysers. There is a squealing in their engines,
the pistons beat on the hoods
like panic trapped in a burning basement,
smoke has risen and leaks out the rusted doors.
The cars crumble to the earth, wheels
spinning in the air, helpless
as turtle legs. The shadows perch
on the axles, folding their wings.
The humming stops like a hand on a tuning fork.
The lights are out, the pistons shattered.
Impassive as commuters, the stars pass without turning.

Translation:

In your eyes, the stars
behind their silent tails
screech like comets,
molten into space. Moons
turn their dark sides
to face your anger.
If you fix on the trees
crouched in the yard,
their bark crackles off,
they bare white skin,
the dying leaves beg
for mercy and shade.
Sand dunes like a force
of hopeless scorpions
surround the house
and sit unmoved as fossils.
Each grain of sand
shatters like a mirror.
Sidewinders scurry
into the emptied street.
The city calls its panicked
fireman home to safety.
They have seen me behind you.
My dragon-tongue is dark,
dark as a spent sun.
It reaches out to cover your eyes.

The
Night
Eyes

Your overnight eyes
wisp thru green
currents like needles, spun thread,
stitch to sea the sea fan,
crouch with a side glance
in a pocket of brain coral.

Like overnight eyes,
the green lids
flick last fins,
drift
by phosphor rays.
At the blue glide,
kelp leans a green stare.

An overnight eye,
sea-blown,
weeps. Anemone
fingers
drum white mercy,
fold over the eye,
stiff, stung.

On a sea night
only skin
barely shells
the night eye in.

Nocturne

We are always in the middle of things,
starting up again
after sleep or a cool drink
under a maple, squinting
as we run our thumbs under
the packs
which trench our shoulders.
While we walk,
to balance our slipping strength
we trail artifacts
heavy with sentiment,
dead as fossils.

We welcome the hound
that rushes through a hedge
to show his redoubtable teeth,
breaking the monotony
of fleeing birds.

At evening we sit by the river,
bottom-fishing, ignoring the teasing bite
of the circling current. As the forest grays
we flee into a noisy sleep.

Paleolithic   The stillness
has breathed
on these stones
is perfectly
natural,
rounded
in a smoothness
of a legend of earth.
They have faded
as men have
into the seasonal depth,
humus taking soil,
soil compacting
in a face of rock,
rock all the while.
We reach for them
hopefully, a right weight
on the palm.
It is a love
settles to the skin,
such gravity as pulls
us down, joined
in the hard thought
of our own slow sinking.

the nature of the place

Pattern
and
Potential

(I)

These cold rocks, out-
crop. Dark basaltic
bed. And the pattern:
intrude, up-lift, fold
and firm.

(II)

　　　We had climbed
above the valley, above
a mud marsh, beyond new
humus, footing
loose on leaves and moss.
Then we sat, tossing twigs
down the hillside,
letting our hearts slow.

We talked of a city, rhythmical.
In counterpoint, harmonious
with this hill, a solidity
of moment. Of the two
as a fused motion, both
thereby, in a realm, human,
ongoing.
　　　And memory:
a herd of sheep
driven slowly from a hill,
thru a clipped pasture land,
to the outer reaches
of the passable roads.

(III)

In a sullen vision
of dead trees, there is
a footpath leading
to a lake. Stunted bluegill
overrun its shallows,
and algae, passive
as a drifting barge,
ride the flat water.
By midsummer
it closes solid below the sun.
The air suspends
like a single blow
on a slack drum.
A man, sentimental, dreaming, ill-at-ease.

(IV)

We had all marched singing,
theatrical, from the forest,
sun on the treetops,
dusk in the valley.
Thru the dark, we had seen
the granite moving
at the cliff side.
Within the outer range
of the thick oaks
and the clustering brush,
it seemed our cooking fire
had re-kindled, that each twig snapping
was a following fire.

(V)

Speaking at the hill crest,
between, a single motion.
Of things made
for a making future
from a dense present.
Of pattern: in hollows
of stone, moss
to staunch a wound;
twigs come to a stop
below the cool hills
and closing rock.
Of men, gathering at dusk
around a fire,
seen from a hill
through a rhythm of branches.

On a
Visit
with
Frank
Samperi

As an angel
would
walk the swirls
of lavaflow,
a circling
of charred
trees—
for where
his eyes
came to be
shone a green.
With cupped
hand
he shaped
a form,
not yet
rock nor dark.
As an angel
would
conceive
a beach
above
a concave sea:
fine
black
sand

Appalachia   Past ten years
                A crane backed slowly thru town,
                Swinging each red rail
                Onto a flatcar
                Like an old woman
                Sweeping the porch.

                Children, shaken
                By the daily anger
                Of their father,
                Sit upon
                The silent ties
                Near the highway,
                Tossing stones.

                Our night is black,
                As an empty house,
                As coal.

The
Forest

Fluid as a man's longing,
A secret shimmers here.
The shadow in a pool,
Beside a rock greased
With algae, flashes
Where the eye is stopped.

Haze leaps from the river
Toward the morning sun.

The
Great
Chain

In the dawn spurt
Of a fish, belly-breaking
From the lurching river,
Single algae
Spend their solar light.

Under the fallen trunk,
Through damp
Humus tunnels,
A salamander breathes
The sun-wave.

Even the mosses
Which quiet
The cold-cracking rocks
Touch in shade
A breeze
Past the patient hawk.

And the night sky
Soaks
In thunderheads.

Valediction   Though we often name the place,
we evoke no longing.
         Streets slick with rain,
         vapor lamps
         coating the rooftops.

    She married
    young.
    At two the son died. I no longer
    take any joy in her memory.

             When we must, we return,
             bored into indolence. If the sentiment
             seemed less naïve, we would be

                       bitter. I

       walked the streets entire,
       through the heavy drizzle,
       her brave tears
       dripping down my coat.

    Still she would never admit
    not enjoying each man.

             Each now must
             somehow believe
             the river clear,
             and the face
             raised to the gods,

returning off the untense
surface. More
pollutes this stream
than this brown flowing
pipeline or any
newly dead.

What of the memory,
fragmented, discontinuous?
There make a picture
acceptable as true?
The spectrum
off the oil slick
light the old love?

Though the place it is

drives us out,
we bear it like
a slave sack.

"You'd best not
come around again,"
he said.

I burned the letters.

We have come past
the tide line.
The salt taste
brings some comfort.

At
Winter's
Edge

Quivering in black circles,
The rippled pond
Scars my face.
Last spring we brought
Pumpkinseed sunfish,
That soon gulped at the frantic air,
And spun to their sides,
Dead as noon.

In the shallows below the path,
Cattails snow the wind,
Oak leaves skid to shore,
The sulphur spring rattles
In its narrow mouth.

Like a moon, a white
Flightless duck
Paddles slowly near the center,
Bleating at the chill sky.
Night will ring its legs
With a glaze of ice.
By morning, the memory
Of the spreading waves
Will pass from the water.

To
My Wife,
Waking
on a
Fall
Morning

Flaked with frost, the maple leaves
Begin to turn. The shriveled sun rises.
A thin breeze thrashes
Through tight, crisping branches.
Stiff at the joints,
The grass is dry. Sap
Steps slowly toward the root.
Like a fist,
The earth creaks shut.

Chill and white, the sharp bones
Of light slant past unused.
Awake together,
Rested beneath thick covers,
The mingled plasm of our blood
Streams to let
No brittle season
Still this harvest warmth.

Poem
in
March

A river thaw
weaves the valley grass.
Silver shad leaf
the kneeling brush.
A dead elm
breaks from the bank.

You look for comfort
into my eyes, tighten
your hand in mine.
We were the single warmth
of winter. Now ice
subsides in riffles at our feet.
Air chatters through the valley.
The sun flames at the low clouds.

We start home.
For all our close love,
by April we will need
more than warmth.

As
If
to
Sleep

As if to sleep,
he drew the window

blinds aside. A low
land fog off the lake.

Garden slugs
churning soft as tongues

below the swings. His wife
calling him back

to make love
silently

riding her back
like a shell.

As Fishes
Do Not Know
They Live
in Water

(I)

Air in scrolls
on the forest floor

carries flakes of granite,
water seeps to the

center of boulders,
falls work upstream,

river over
rounded pebbles.

(II)

Boulders crack in the valley.
Under wind

branches sweep to earth.
Deer break ice

to drink.
Snow cuts under

the sill of the door.

The 8:25 to New York — Written on the First Day of Rosh Hashana

The vine leaves
of the poison ivy
are turning red.
They have spiraled up
the willow and down
the hanging branches
pointing back
toward the earth
and the train I am riding.
The mountains are green.
Only an early,
morning haze assumes
a change. A slow creek scours
this valley. Hunger,
like a prod,
coils minnows near the surface,
a lone duck dabbing
patiently at the water.
Then sumac,
sprawling toward the tracks,
a half-empty parking lot
still behind.
Spinning out,
toward the tracks,
the city
will not hear yet
of willow
or of fall.
Underground thru Harlem,
we ride
the last mile of mercy.

5730

Grand
Central

She will not outlast
the winter,
sits against a wall,
reading the news,
her legs, rough
as unglazed clay,
wrapped in bandages.
In bedroom slippers
she shuffles down a ramp,
holding a shopping bag.

The
Locations

(I)

The place
landlocked

past any sense
of water

but the torpid.
The green

sumac, long leaves
flourishing.

A yellow tinge
takes

the thick river—
fish, muddy, inedible.

Scant pull
of ocean

as if
tides

could stretch
so far.

(II)

Swallowed alive
by the sea

yearly the salmon,
red and sleek,

gather in estuaries
aging years

as they climb
upstream

to lay eggs
in fresh water.

They are dead
before the eggs

can hatch. The fry
catching a certain

clear smell
of river,

sweep
out of their element

into
their element.

There is no
tracing them

or the year.

Letter to an
Inland Friend:
The Lower
Hudson.
— To
Doris Eder

You can guess
my surprise.

For the oil surface,
the half-sunken

logs, spilled
from the docks—

killifish persist
in this water,

glass chips,
spinning on the solid current,

some
reaching four inches.

Well below
the surface,

blind, schooled
sharks

feed on rubbish
washed

over the river floor.
Seagulls

stalk the air.
Silent and scarce,

they survive
on killifish.

**I Come
to a Pier
on a
Winter Night,
Thinking
of the
Cold**

Should it hold,
high in the cheeks—

the long wind
turned aside,

ears
too hot to touch,

each breath
alight, slow.

On the river,
lights along the wave-tips

coming, watched,
to a boil

at the shoreline,
a deep

roil
farther out.

My eyes
now

too full to close.
Should it hold

this night,
thick with inversion,

should you reach
to touch my face,

you will melt,
alive.

The
Killer
Whale

By all accounts,
the killer whale
is a largely docile
animal, drawn to man
by curiosity. There are
no verified cases
of killer whales
attacking a man, though
the earlier name "whale
killers" indicates
they prey on the sick and weak
of other species. Many
consider them superior
in intelligence to the dolphin
since they exhibit no
antipathy to trainers
when captured. At the prospect
of a free fish they
may allow a trainer
to place his head inside
their mouth, holding teeth
curved inward for tearing.
In the wild they reach
forty feet.
The blue whale, however,
reaching a hundred feet,
is nearly extinct.
Pale blue, it strains
the ocean
for a small shrimp,
spouting after years
below the ice,

feeling the whaleboats
tremble. Though its heartbeat
has been monitored
no one has dared
to gauge
its intelligence.

After
the
Community's
Dream

(1)

In the clipped
line, the
stunted phrase.

Forever west,
unbroken
lines, gap

east to west
like arrows.
He stood

exhausted, above
a high ridge,
facing the sea,

sun
setting
in his eyes,

a Mayan
calendar. No
reason

left to tell it
over. Finding
the way

thru, they
crowd
as pilgrims

to the California
coast, braving
completion.

(II)

Heyerdahl, crossing
the ocean, finding
tar bobbing

in mid-
Atlantic,
left

the sinking
raft,
still

trying
to prove
the feat:

Egypt, drifting
west
as far as faith,

undaunted.

(III)

Sampling
the wild grapes,
they

struggled
home in dragon-
boats, lost

the
pleasant
empty place.

(IV)

Such
as
it is,

the
point
made.

A strain
on
tradition

the moon
is
dulled.

There is no
panic
to speak of.

The
Nature
of the
Place:
Coda

It is
the

nature
of the place

to continue.
No man

to stop
this motion.

No man
at all.

A sun
will heat

evermore
this earth,

moon
reach

out
for sea,

the stars'
control

as remote.
Man

to continue,
no

matter
lost,

his skin
splitting open

like
an egg case.